The Power of Presence

Helping People Help People

by Doug Manning

In-Sight Books

Helping People Help People

Oklahoma City, Oklahoma

In-Sight Books

First Printing
February 2004

Copyright© 2004 by In-Sight Books, Inc.
P. O. Box 42467
Oklahoma City, Oklahoma 73123
800.658.9262 or 405.810.9501
www.insightbooks.com

Manufactured in the United States of America

ISBN 1-892785-53-6

Cover Photo:
Digital Imagery© 2004 Getty Images

Quotes:
Zadra, Dan and Marcia Woodard, comp. *Forever Remembered.*
Seattle: Compendium, Inc., 1997. ISBN 1-888387-20-3
Cobb, Nancy. *In Lieu of Flowers: A Conversation for the Living.*
New York: Pantheon Books, 2001. ISBN 0-375-71448-0
McNees, Pat, ed. *Dying: A Book of Comfort.*
Garden City, NY: Warner Books, 1996. ISBN 0-446-67400-1
Cook, John, comp. *The Book of Positive Quotations.*
Minneapolis: Fairview Press, 1993.
ISBN 1-57749-053-3

Contents

Preface

Almost forty years ago, a book by John Drakeford titled *The Awesome Power of the Listening Ear* skinned my eyes so I could see. From that moment on, I have been trying to write this book. It has taken all of these years to fill out the concepts I first discovered in that book. I began by experiencing the dynamics of small groups. As I began to explore my feelings, and the feelings of some brave people who chose to share with me, I discovered more and more applications to the power of listening.

A few months ago, quite by accident, I stumbled onto the analogy of the buckets. From that moment on, the book wrote itself.

As with all of the books I have written, I must thank my wife for fifty years of constant and loving support. I must also thank the staff of In-Sight Books. Their care and talent make writing a relaxed joy. What I mess up, they fix.

My hope is that someone reading this book will discover the wonderful experience of the power of listening.

Doug Manning
August 27, 2003

Section ONE
Can We Talk?

Needed: A strong, deep person wise enough to
allow me to grieve in the depth of who I am, and strong enough to hear
my pain without turning away. I need someone who believes that the
sun will rise again, but who does not fear my darkness. Someone who
can point out the rocks in my way without making me a
child by carrying me. Someone who can stand
in thunder and watch the lightning and
believe in a rainbow.

–Fr. Joe Mahoney
Concerns of Police Survivors newsletter

Can We Talk?

Within days of the September 11, 2001, horrors, the phones in our office began to ring. We heard the same request over and over for days on end, "What can we say to these people?" The whole world was overwhelmed and searching for help. It seemed as if everyone felt like it was time for them to talk and no one knew what to say.

Times of great and sudden tragedy make that need much more acute, but we face something very similar almost every day. There is rarely a time when someone we know is not facing pain. A friend is getting a divorce. A family is in great struggle with a child out of control. Someone we know has just lost a loved one. A family is going through the devastation of a suicide. A family member has been diagnosed with cancer or Alzheimer's disease. Maybe the most frightening of all—someone very close is dying.

"What do you say to someone in pain?" is not just a question we ask after some national tragedy. It is a question we face every day of our lives. That is especially true if our work brings us into intimate contact with people. All caregiving professionals face this issue on an hourly basis. What do we say to people?

One of the amazing discoveries of my life has been that just because people work in caregiving environments does not guarantee that they know what to say or how to respond to people in pain.

A funeral director pulled me aside and quietly said, "I have been a funeral director for eighteen years, and I have no idea what to say to families when they walk into my office."

I cannot count the number of nurses, hospital chaplains, clergy, physicians, social workers, hospice workers, and others in these types of occupations who have expressed the same kind of fears and helpless feelings.

One visit with a person in grief will reveal that the vast majority of us have no idea what to say nor how to react to people in grief or pain. Most report that, not only do people say the wrong things but, too often, their friends avoid them because they do not know what to say. Almost everyone who suffers the death of a loved one will also suffer the loss of friends. The friends mean well and certainly do not wish to say the wrong things. They do not want to avoid their friends in their time of need, but they have no idea what to say.

My hope for this book is not that I will provide some magic words for you to say. My hope is that we can have an honest conversation about the needs and the frustrations we feel in trying to meet those needs, and together build a new pattern that will help people heal. You will hear me say over and over that people in grief need safe people. My hope for this book is that we will discover ways to be safe people.

This book is written in a personal voice. I visualize this as just the two of us talking about a mutual concern. There is nothing clinical in this book. I am not that smart. Everything I know about grief comes from what someone has told me or what I have experienced myself. Everything I know about people has been taught to me by people. I am not an expert; I am just a person who has traveled around listening to people's stories. I am here to share with you what these stories have taught me.

So let's talk together about dealing with people in pain. Maybe the best place to start would be a survey of how you react and what you are most likely to say. This is not a trap. I am not going to spend the rest of the book trying to prove you wrong. This is just an honest attempt to help you see what is happening now and then to compare it with anything you happen to learn from my stories. I have provided some space for you to write down your responses to some situations. I hope you will take this seriously enough to pause and write.

I was leading a conference on anger and guilt in grief, and I asked the group what they felt guilty about. One young mother said, "All the way to the hospital my son begged me to turn around. He did not want the transplant. He was afraid. I would not turn around, and he died." What would you say to that mother?

You were only doing what you thought was the absolute best thing for him. Jesus has him now. You will see him again. Please don't blame yourself. Your decision was motivated by love.

A friend of mine just called. He has been diagnosed with inoperable cancer. He has a hypochondriac sort of personality, so I don't know whether his story is really as bad as he is making it sound. He is highly excitable on his best days, so you can imagine how upset he is on the phone. What should I say? How should I respond?

What are you feeling right now? Are you okay? I'm sorry you have to go through this. Do you want to pray? Please tell me what you would like God to do for you?

You bump into a person at the grocery store. You know her fairly well, although you are not close friends. This is the first time you have seen her since her daughter was murdered. Her daughter was a very talented person with a great career ahead of her, but she struggled with substance abuse and was murdered while buying drugs. What do you say? Would you duck down another aisle to avoid saying anything? How nervous would this make you?

> I would casualy walk up to her.
> With soft eyes & a gentle smile
> say "hi, It's good to see you..
> Have you been okay?
> If you want to talk or
> get together sometime, just
> let me know.

Your loved one is terminally ill. You know the condition, and even though you have not talked, your loved one also knows the truth. Talking about death is the ultimate intimacy. Could you do it? Would you avoid it at all cost and tell yourself it is better if it is not acknowledged? How would you respond?

> Yes. We need to talk about
> this (touching their arm
> or shoulder) Is now okay?
> What are you thinking?

Grab A Bucket

This may sound rather childish, and you may feel strange doing so, but find a couple of small paint buckets. If you do not have any buckets, then a water pitcher will do or a couple of bowls. Anything that will hold liquids will be fine. Since I use buckets when I am talking about this, I will refer to buckets, and you can make the translation.

Pick up one of the buckets and imagine that you are the young mother whose son needed a transplant, and she would not turn back. Try to place yourself in her mind and heart and then write down what is in her bucket. What is she feeling? Granted, there is no way to really know or understand all of the hurts that are there, but we can at least grasp some general ideas. We do not need to completely understand. Our aim here is to simply focus on her bucket. What is in her bucket? Write out what you see before you read further.

_____

_____

_____

_____

_____

_____

_____

_____

_____

_____

_____

I am doing this activity as I write, so I can report what I see in the bucket:

> I see a great deal of anger that has no place to go. I see lone-liness because she cannot find anyone who will concentrate on her bucket. There is also loneliness because she cannot make even her spouse understand how she feels. She is trying to explain her feelings and all she has to do that with are words. There are no words for these kinds of feelings.

> I see fear, fear that some other tragedy may come, and one more will be too much to bear. I see guilt that goes all the way back to the birth of her son. Was his heart condition her fault? Did she do something wrong during her pregnancy? Was it her genes that did it? Rational or not, something must be blamed and, too often, the blame turns inward.

> I see despair. Her son has been dead for over four years, and the pain is still fresh and intense. Will she ever be well? Will she ever laugh again? Will she ever enjoy life without a tinge of guilt?

Now pick up the other bucket. That bucket is yours. When you are standing facing this young mother, what is in your bucket? What are you feeling?

> I am feeling fear. I don't want to get into her bucket. What if it all gets out of control? What if I get in over my head? What if it goes on and on? I have an appointment in a few moments, so I don't have time for a long, drawn-out session. She needs more than I can give. She should go get professional help. There is nothing I can do. All of that says I am afraid of the intimacy, so I make up all kinds of reasons to stay out of her bucket.

I also have all kinds of advice in my bucket: Clever sayings, scriptures, new ways to look at what happened and put a positive spin on it, and encouraging words to get her to put this all behind her and move on.

The problem is that her bucket is already full. There is no room for any of the stuff in my bucket. No matter how great it is, until some of the feelings that fill her bucket are worked out, her bucket cannot receive anything else. We keep pouring it in, but it does no good.

Now try the buckets with the other people we listed. When we really look at the buckets, it becomes clear that trying to pour our stuff into their buckets will not help and often might do harm. How, then, do we help people?

I am convinced that the only way to help people is to get into their buckets and listen to them. That may not sound dramatic or even adequate, but the ear is the most powerful part of the human body, and people in pain need presence more than they need information. I often say there is no such thing as grief therapy. People in grief need a friend more than they need a counselor. There are certainly those in grief that need therapy, but the need for therapy was not caused by the grief. The need was there before the grief. The loss may have made the need more acute, but the vast majority of people who are walking through grief need a companion, not a therapist. I do not do therapy. I am not equipped to do so. This book is not aimed at helping you do therapy. The goal is to become equipped to be a safe companion.

Listening without giving advice or even making a comment sounds rather inadequate. When I tell grieving people that they need to find some safe people and "talk grief to death," some express doubt that just talking will help them in their struggle. All of us have experienced the power of the ear, but, somehow, when the chips are down for someone else, we tend to think talking works better than listening.

There is no greater loan than a sympathetic ear.
–Frank Tyger

Notes

_____

_____

_____

_____

_____

_____

_____

_____

_____

_____

_____

_____

_____

_____

_____

_____

_____

_____

_____

_____

_____

_____

_____

_____

Ears And Learning

I told a well-known evangelist that I was a divine healer. I don't think he heard me, but I said, "You want to lay hands on people, and I want to lay ears on them. I really think there is power in the ear." There are some things that happen to people when we "lay ears on them" that cannot happen in any other method of healing. May I share a few of them with you?

We have all heard that we cannot learn with our mouths open. There is a myth that learning can only happen as we listen while someone pours gems of wisdom into us. The myth is wrong. We learn as we talk. Learning almost demands that we talk. When we get a thought, it remains "head knowledge" until we have a chance to speak that thought out loud. Then it internalizes and becomes a part of us. Too often our system of education is based on just the opposite of that. We are supposed to learn while someone lectures to us, and we take it all in or take it down in notes. Unless there is the chance for feedback, the information is just dates and figures that are not a part of us.

We can only remember ten percent of what anyone says. We can remember ninety percent of what we say while we are doing something. At seminars I often ask the people in my audience to tell me who they are and what they do. Then I ask them to tell whether they are "innies" or "outies." I am not talking about navels. I am talking about the roll of tissue in the rest room. Some people want the roll put on the spindle so the paper comes over the top away from the wall. Others want it to go toward the wall and out the bottom. The over the toppers are the "outies." The underneath ones are the "innies." The strange thing is that almost everyone has an opinion about toilet paper. We have a great time arguing the merits of both methods, and we hear from a small minority who couldn't care less. Then I say, "Six months from now, you will have a hard time remembering my name. You think you will remember the jokes I tell, but you won't. You will write down the punch lines and forget the rest. However, you will remember what you said when you told us whether you were an 'innie' or an 'outie' from now on. You will remember because you remember what you say while you are doing something. That is learning."

Helping people involves simply listening while they learn. The problem is that we cannot determine what they learn. Nor can we set the pace of their learning. We cannot know what they learn, which is even more disconcerting. Getting in their bucket means we let them learn what they choose, when they are ready. Don't think that will be easy. You are getting ready for some major tongue biting and wondering if anything is being done that will ever be of help. Companioning is a most frustrating experience, to say the least. Frustrating, but effective.

Ears And Insight

I have never understood how counseling works, even though I have been involved in counseling for most of my adult life. I have studied people and the way we respond to life more than any other subject. I still have no idea how I can sit with my chin in my hand and mumble every once in a while and then people get better. After forty years, I am always amazed when progress happens.

The only explanation is that insight happens to people when they talk and when someone listens. Somehow the talking clears out the barriers, and they suddenly see and understand more about what they are feeling than you or I could ever tell them.

I have watched this phenomenon happen again and again when I have the good sense to just listen to people. I saw a dramatic illustration of this with a woman who happened to be a motor mouth. She was very nervous and afraid of counseling. She hid her fears behind constant talk. Usually a person who is trying to control the counseling by talking will calm down after a session or so, and a normal conversation can happen. This lady never stopped. She would talk session after session. About all I ever said to her was "Good morning." During one session, insight hit her. She stopped in mid-sentence and said, "You know, I think I have always felt like I had to compete with my mother." I did not say a word. She mulled the thought over in her mind for a while and then talked the rest of the hour. At the next session, I asked her not to talk until I had a chance to ask her a question. Surprisingly, she agreed. I asked her what she had learned in our sessions. She immediately said, "Last time when *you told me* I had to compete with my mother, that was profound." I guess I needed some credit, so I did not tell her that the insight had come from her and not me.

The difference between counseling and companioning is found in this concept. Counseling is a valid and valuable resource for the many people who need help in discovering the causes of their struggles. Companioning works more like a catalyst. We do not direct the process nor suggest the course. We simply listen and allow insights to happen. They happen because the catalyst of a listening ear helps make that possible.

I have watched in wonder as people in grief find an insight that works for them on their own. Often, they will tell me some new way of thinking they have discovered that somehow helped them turn the corner in the way they cope. Sometimes, I must shake my head at some of the things they say. I have to remind myself that it is their insight, and it works for them even if doesn't make sense to me at all.

Many years ago a person told me that he could not get past the death of his daughter. Then the thought hit him that if someone had told him before she was born that he would only have her for sixteen years he would have immediately said that he wanted her for as long as possible, regardless of the time limit. I thought since that worked for him, it would work for others as well. I tried it on the next family whose child had died, and they looked at me like I had lost my mind. Insight has to come from within. Others' insights do not heal. They may encourage. They may cause someone to think. Insights that heal must come from the hearts and the minds of the people in pain. We allow that to happen when we realize we are a catalyst and when we simply listen.

The problem is, we cannot control what insights people find. We cannot test or even evaluate what is happening inside of those we listen to. This means we will never feel very adequate in our work. I leave every session wondering if anything good has happened. I am companioning a mother whose daughter was murdered. We meet every week and have done so for almost two years. Last week, I walked her to the car and wondered if the session had been a waste of time. I have wondered that every session for two years. Helping people always leaves us feeling inadequate. All we can do is hold on and wait for insight.

Ears And Anger

All of us have experienced a time of anger that could not be expressed. We stewed and seethed for days on end with no relief. Then we told someone what we were angry about, and somehow we couldn't make it seem as bad as it was. We felt silly to have been so upset, and we finally said, "Well, you had to be there." If you have ever had such an experience, then you know the power the listening ear has in dissipating anger.

Psychologists suggest that <u>anger must be expressed</u>. I would add that anger needs someone to say it and someone to hear it. It does no good to say it if no one is really listening. As a matter of fact, the anger grows until it is heard by a sympathetic ear. <u>It must be heard</u>.

Hearing anger is one of our toughest assignments. We have an almost overwhelming urge to explain it all away. We almost inevitably become spin doctors trying to put the best face on the situation. Then we leave with the person's anger still in force and feeling totally inadequate. Anger is gradually bled off by the power of a listening ear. The person may not seem better when you walk away, but if he has vented, he has been helped. You will not experience many miraculous or sudden healings in your lifetime. Change comes one silly millimeter at a time.

Ears And Understanding

My daughters claim that I only know three words, and I have written thirty books about them. They may be right. If they are right, one of those three words is "understanding." The longer I live, the more I walk with people in pain, the more I believe that, we all want to be understood. Someone giving credence to our thoughts and legitimizing our feelings not only makes us feel good, it is also healing.

For example, if a woman comes into my office and says, "I don't love my husband anymore. I have no reason for that lack of feeling. He has not done anything that I can put my finger on, but I woke up one day and realized I had lost a great deal of my feelings for him, and I can't seem to get them back." It is amazing how often this condition traces back to a woman who has never been understood. Every time she had a thought, she was told either in words, attitude or body language, "That's wrong," or, "That's stupid." Every time she expressed feelings, she was told either in words, attitude or body language, "That's silly," or, "Isn't that just like a woman?" Every time that happened, she felt diminished. That diminishing does not go away. It builds up inside until it finally chokes off feelings. She is left wondering what happened to her feelings.

All of us have feelings too deep for expressing that we would give anything for someone to just understand. My wife gives me permission to tell her story. She had both of her breasts removed several years ago. She had multiple fibroid tumors, and had a double mastectomy to protect her from cancer. No one prepared her for the full impact of this kind of surgery. No one told her how painful it would be, nor that reconstruction is a long way from how she looked before the surgery. A few years after her surgery, I asked her what she really felt during those days. She said, "I woke up every morning thinking, 'I am going to go back to that doctor and tell him he made a mistake and to put them back.'" When I asked her why she did not say that, she replied, "Where would you go to say that? You know what the answer would be. They would just say 'they can't do that' and what good would that be?" But wouldn't it be wonderful if there were a place where you could go and say that? Just having someone understand would be healing.

A woman told me the story of dealing with the death of her son. She said:

> My son died. There was a party with some drinking, and someone had a gun. The gun went off, and my son died. I had a terrible time with the word *accident*. An accident is when cars wreck or lightning strikes. If a guy has a gun in his hand with his finger on the trigger and the gun goes off, it is more than an accident. When I would say that, everyone would immediately think I thought my son was murdered. I would say that I did not think that, but they could not see what I was trying to say. I was caught between words and could not find anyone who could understand. I could not get past that need. I could not begin to deal with my grieving. All I

could think about was that word. I finally went to see one of my son's friends who was at the party. The friend happened to be a paraplegic confined to a wheelchair. When I entered the room, he was very tense. He had both arms up in front of his chest like he needed protection. When I said that I was having a hard time with the word accident, he lowered his arms, let out a sigh and said, "So am I." That's all it took. I began to get well that day.

Someone understood.

If we can be understood, we can move on. If we cannot be understood, we tend to park there, and the need for understanding becomes an obsession to us. I have spent a long time studying long term hurts and grudges. A grudge doesn't happen because someone is too hardheaded to forgive. A grudge happens when someone is hurt and cannot get that hurt accepted or understood. Gradually, the need for understanding becomes an obsession and can color the entire life of a person.

A young woman grabbed me after a recent speech and said, "My seven year-old daughter died, and I have waited eight years to hear someone say what you just said." With that she almost collapsed into my arms and began to sob. The crowd did not know what to do or how to relate, so they stood in stunned silence while she wept. Finally, she looked up and said, "Thank you; I feel so much better. It is like a heavy load has been lifted from me, and I am free."

That story sounds melodramatic, to say the least, but those kinds of experiences happen quite often. They do not happen because I am a charismatic speaker; they happen because people feel like someone finally understands what they are feeling. The search is over; they have been understood.

It must be said here that there is no way for us to really understand someone else. They are trying to share feelings and all they have to do that with are words. There are no words that can adequately do that. We cannot understand and we should not say that we know exactly how they feel. Using understanding to heal others involves taking a position of acceptance. Whatever they feel, we should try to get into those feelings with them instead of trying to clearly see everything we are told. It is getting in their buckets, whether we see it or not.

Speaking of buckets, go back and pick up your bucket again, and let's look at the woman who did not turn back from the transplant. During the seminar, I asked her how many times someone had told her that she was acting out of love. She said she could not count the times. I asked her if that had helped, and she said "no." I asked her how many times someone had told her that her son would have died without the transplant, and I received the same answer. Then I asked how many people had told her it had been long enough, and she should get on with her life. To that she said, not only did it not help, but it also made her very angry.

Then I said, "What if I came over there and hugged you and said, 'That must really hurt.' Would that help?" She said that it would help a lot. That is what she was looking for. Someone to simply get into her bucket and try to understand where she was instead of trying to change her. "That must really hurt" is one of the most healing phrases I know.

The opposite of understanding is not misunderstanding. The opposite is "trivialization." The best way for us to discuss this issue is for you to pick up your bucket again. Let's say you are the father of a nine-year-old daughter killed in a car wreck. I am your friend, and I have come to give you comfort. Think about what you would be feeling and what you would want from me. Your bucket is full of hurt, anger, loneliness, despair, and you feel totally unable to express what you feel. You cling to the pain. You want someone who will simply understand where you are and what you feel. Someone who will understand without you having to explain. There is no way you could possibly explain, and you don't have the energy.

I come along and say, "God won't put more on you than you can bear."

How does that make you feel? I have just told you that what you are suffering is no big deal. I have told you to "buck up and get over it," I just used religious terms to do so. Does that help?

Or, I say, "Think of how lucky you are to have had her for nine years." Does that make any of the pain go away?

What if I said, as a person actually did say to a friend of mine, "Perhaps your daughter would have grown up to be a bad person, and God took her home before she could be bad." Does that make it all better? Or are you ready to throw furniture?

Most of the help people receive in grief must come from their friends. Unfortunately, a great deal of the hurt will also come from their friends. Our efforts to cheer people up too often trivialize their grief right at the time they are desperate for someone to understand.

I had cancer a few years ago. Prior to the surgery, I became so tired of being trivialized that I would no longer tell people about the cancer. It hurt when they would dismiss my problem with some passing statement about how sure they were that I would be fine. I really got tired of promises to pray for me. I even had one person say, "Aren't you glad you have the good kind of cancer." Talk about an oxymoron! There are no good cancers. One day I needed to talk to someone. I had already worn my wife's ears out, so I called a friend of mine. I have known this person all of her life. She is from my home town, and I have always loved her because she is different and delightfully crazy. I called and said, "I have cancer." She said, "Oh! S--t." and began to cry. After a little while, she caught herself and said, "Oh! I am so sorry. I should not have said that to you, and I should not be crying. I should be cheering you up." I said, "Hush, you are messing up the only appropriate response I have gotten so far." Having someone hurt with me felt wonderful. Not having any explanations or platitudes thrown at me was healing.

This even applies to the use of scripture. I love the Bible, and I try to live by its principles, but, too often, the scriptures we love to quote to people in pain are the ones that trivialize their pain. We can tell someone *all things work together for good* twenty years after the event, but to say that the morning after someone dies is trivializing instead of comforting.

If you have been able to feel what is in the bucket of a grieving father, then it should be evident that all of the efforts to take away the pain, end up adding to the problem. Hopefully you can also see how helpful it is when someone gets in the bucket with a person and tries to simply understand.

Ears And Significance

Now we come to my very favorite word. The reason understanding works is that when we are understood we can establish the significance of the loss or the hurt. The most natural response to any event in our lives is the desire to establish the significance of that event. Almost every book I have written has a section on significance. When bad things happen to us, we want someone to know about it, and we want them to acknowledge how bad or hurtful that event really is.

Because I talk about significance so much, I notice people looking for it all around me: A woman in an airport announcing to everyone on a shuttle bus that she hopes the plane is on time because she is flying to the funeral for her mother. Total strangers in hospitals telling me why they are there. "My son is having surgery today," or, "My wife's been in here for three weeks, and it is just one thing after another." Establishing significance is the most human thing I know.

If we can establish significance, we can move on. If we cannot, we tend to park there and build an obsession the same way we do if we cannot be understood. Most of the time, healing cannot start until someone enters into our pain with us and sees the real impact of the event on our lives.

It becomes evident that people need people when they hurt. It also becomes evident that people need a certain kind of person when they hurt.

Honest listening is one of the best medicines we can offer the dying and the bereaved.
–Jean Cameron

Notes

_____

_____

_____

_____

_____

_____

_____

_____

_____

_____

_____

_____

_____

_____

_____

_____

_____

_____

_____

_____

_____

_____

Laying Ears On 'Em

When we combine understanding with significance, we have developed a wonderfully healing team, but it may not seem so at first. The idea of just listening to people cuts across our background and rearing. We may need to get rid of some of the myths of our childhood before we can become comfortable with the "being in the bucket" approach to healing. Some of us were raised to think:

Myth #1
Sympathy Makes It Worse

That was certainly the prevailing idea of my youth. "If we sympathize with people, they will just get worse. They don't need our pity. Heaven knows they are showing enough pity without our adding to it." Our job was to cheer them up or tell them some nice platitude that would make them feel better. Trivialization was born out of our fear of sympathy.

Myth #2
Tears Are Corrosive

Most of us do not do well with tears. The moment someone begins to cry, we either feel an urge to run or an urge to try to make them stop crying. "Now, don't cry," is embedded in our psyches, and it is embedded deep. Learning how to walk with people while they cry takes long and hard practice. It will not be easy.

Myth #3
Stoicism Is Strength

I wish Jackie Kennedy had cried at her husband's funeral. We all have that picture of her and John Jr. standing on the steps of the Capitol— John Jr. saluting and his mother standing there with head up and not a tear. The whole nation seemed to think they were seeing the epitome of handling grief with dignity and class. That is almost the national model for public grieving. Classy people are strong. To be stoic in the face of grief is something to be admired. Consequently, every widow feels she must apologize for her tears. How often does someone cry without saying they are sorry?

Myth #4
We Can Change The Way Someone Feels By Changing The Way They Think

Cognitive Therapy certainly has its place in healing, but it also must be said that feelings do not always follow thought. It needs to be said again that we are not developing a counseling or therapeutic model here. We need to leave that to those who are trained. For our work, it is important to know that just giving someone a new way to think does not automatically give him a new way to feel. Our whole society seems to be built on the idea that it will do so. Product advertising and self-improvement books all are aimed at the single concept that if a person thinks or looks at life in a different way, then he will feel better looking, sexier, healthier and ready to conquer the world and forget any problems that he had.

The drive to cure by thought is very strong. It seems to have created a natural pattern for how we deal with people in pain. There are three steps to the pattern.

We Explain

The moment some tragic event or death happens, we seem to have an instinctive need to explain why. After years of dealing with people in pain, I still catch myself fighting the urge. We seem to cling to the idea that if they could just understand why it happened, the pain would go away or at least not hurt so bad.

This urge creates some of the horrible things people say when there is a death or a tragedy. Can you imagine that guy telling my friend his child might have grown up to be a bad person? The person who said that is not a bad person. He was trying to help. He just saw explanation as the way to help.

We Argue

If explanation does not work, we argue. "Now you can't let yourself feel like that." "You know there was nothing you could do." "You cannot blame yourself." "You need to get in control." "You must calm yourself down." I could go on and on. We seem to feel uncomfortable with their tears, so we begin a verbal barrage trying to get them to stop.

We Criticize

If explanation and argument fail, we criticize. "You are not trying to get well." "You are wallowing in your grief and just feeling sorry for yourself." "It is time for you to put this behind you and get on with your life."

The pattern is Explain, Argue, Criticize. I thought I was pretty smart when I discovered that pattern; then I reread the book of Job in the Bible. Job was a wealthy man with a large family. He lost everything—his family, his possessions and his health. Three friends came to see Job when he was in agony. They spoke in turn. The first one explained. The second one argued. The third one criticized. The pattern is as old as human nature. It may be old, but it still does not work.

*Don't try to be too wise; don't always try to search for something
profound to say. You don't have to do or say anything to
make things better. Just be there as fully as you can.
And if you are feeling a lot of anxiety and fear and
don't know what to do, admit that openly to the
person you are with and ask his or her help.*

–Sogyal Rinpoche
The Tibetan Book of Living and Dying

Notes

_____

_____

_____

_____

_____

_____

_____

_____

_____

_____

_____

_____

_____

_____

_____

_____

_____

_____

_____

_____

_____

The Healing Pattern

Knowing what not to say or how not to react is not enough. We need to discover a new pattern of reacting if we are to become the comforters we want and need to be. I do not have any magic that will suddenly turn us into great listening companions to those who hurt. I do think there are three keys toward that goal.

Comfort

The hardest part of listening may be getting comfortable just listening. We don't think we have done anything until we have said something. We tend to fear that the people we are trying to help will think we aren't smart enough to have anything to say, or even worse, that we do not care and are not interested enough to try. Learning how to be comfortable will be a continuing struggle as you work with people. I have been working on it for years, and I still must tell myself it is all right to be quiet. Sometimes I tell myself that *after* I have spoken instead of before. The natural thing is to talk.

In a recent conference, a grieving mother said:

> The person who helped me the most when my son died was a friend who never said very much at all. I would call her with some off-the-wall statement about my son's death. She would listen and then say that I was absolutely right. The next day I would call her with something that contradicted everything I had said the day before, and she would say that I was right. The third day I might contradict everything I said both days before, and she would say

that I was absolutely right. She was not there to direct me; she just wanted to hear and love me as I struggled with my off-the-wall stuff.

Remember, we are companioning until they reach their own insights and answers. What we think or what we say is not the issue. All we can do is be a catalyst that helps them react to their feelings in a more comfortable way. When we simply accept and allow them to establish significance, then we have done it.

When I was young there was a cleaners in our town named 'Nuf Said Cleaners. I love that name. It is hard to realize that when we listen, that is 'nuf said.

Focus

We have already discussed how hard it is to get into someone else's bucket. No one can be focused totally on someone else. The most we can hope for is to share our focus, to make an honest effort to see and understand what someone else is feeling. I know of no way to do this other than by learning to grab ourselves by the nape of the neck and forcing the issue.

Focusing outside of ourselves is not natural. Most of the time we are focusing on ourselves. We tend to worry about how we are being perceived, how we look, or how we sound. A good question is, "What is my mind doing while someone else is talking?" Most of the time we are thinking about what we are going to say when they stop talking instead of actually making the effort to hear what they are saying and what they are not saying.

Often, we develop habits that are not conducive to listening. I have asked quite a number of people what their minds do when they are not actively engaged in some activity that demands their attention. The answers were very revealing. One person said that she types in her mind. While someone is talking, she is concentrating on typing what they say. Like most good typists, she is typing the words but not thinking about the meaning. Another person said he spelled the last word in each sentence. One person spelled the last word in each sentence backwards. I tend to line things up with my foot. All of these are habits that must be broken if we are to focus. It takes time. It takes effort. It takes practice. That is why I suggest you actually get a real bucket and make the effort of imagining what the people in this book are feeling. That is a good way to practice focus.

Timing

It is not what you say, nor how you say it that matters. It is *when* you say it. You can say almost anything you wish after someone knows you have heard him, and he will not be offended. There is a place for your input, but it is always after. There is a place for your prayers, scriptures, thoughts, and poems, but it must be after he knows you have heard him. Anything you say before that can be offensive. Even good things can be heard completely wrong. It is not the words; it is the timing.

I wrote a little book called *Socks* because one of the top issues in nursing homes is lost socks. I interviewed several nursing home administrators and found out that lost socks is one of the major complaints, and it hit me that socks could not be the real issue. People have been losing socks for as long as there have been socks. I think the manufacturers make one of every pair of socks water soluble, and the things melt. I tried to figure out what was behind the lost socks. I came up with this scenario.

A woman is giving care to her mother who is a resident of a nursing home. Her brothers are no help and constantly criticize the care she gives, even though they do not do anything to help. Her husband complains daily about the time and effort she must spend in caring for her mother. They have not had a day off in a year, much less a vacation. Every time she goes to see her mother, she gets a load of guilt from Mom about how bad the treatment is and how unhappy she is to be forced to live in such a place.

One night both brothers call and unload. Her husband reacts to her being upset by jumping on her because she spends too much time caring for her mother. She does not sleep all night. The next morning nothing goes right. She burns the toast; she drops an egg on the floor. She continues the fight with her husband that started the night before. The car starts and then dies when she puts it in gear. A few times like that will make a person lose her religion. She arrives at the nursing home absolutely wiped out, and her mother tells her that they lost her socks in the laundry. The first thing she knows, she is in the administrator's office bouncing off the walls about lost socks.

This is a good time to practice. Pick up your bucket and become that woman. What is she feeling? What is she wanting? What will help her?

_____

_____

_____

_____

_____

_____

_____

Pick up the other bucket and become the administrator. What is he or she feeling? What does he or she want to do? Try to focus on their feelings at that moment.

_____

_____

_____

_____

_____

_____

_____

_____

_____

If the administrator responds to the socks issue, they have a long and hot conversation about the wrong things. Anger is a strange animal. It expresses itself in hidden language. Usually people get mad in public about things they think are safe and hide the real issues that are behind the anger. We are all like a mother quail acting wounded to lead the dog away from the nest. We do not let people into our nest until we know they are safe. We discover whether or not they are safe by exploding over extraneous issues first.

If the administrator will listen through the socks, then the woman will begin telling all of the other things that she has been mad about and never voiced. If that is listened through, then she will let the administrator into her bucket. She will begin to talk about what is happening to her. There are a couple of other things about anger. Anger grows until someone is sorry. Most of the time, all people want to hear is, "I am sorry that happened to you." Then anger peaks. It will build and build and then gradually peak and begin to subside. *After* it peaks, you can speak. That is timing. We speak when it is time for us to speak, and then, and only then, will we really be heard.

I am here. Let's heal together.
–A Friend

Notes

_____

_____

_____

_____

_____

_____

_____

_____

_____

_____

_____

_____

_____

_____

_____

_____

_____

_____

_____

_____

The Personal Bucket

While this book is about helping people in pain, the concept of being in someone else's bucket has applications in almost every area of our lives.

Relationships with your spouse or significant other could be strengthened, and peace could be found in this simple act of focusing on the other person. Most arguments result in two people trying to explain what is in their buckets at the same time, and neither one is being heard. Can you imagine the result if your mate simply tried to feel what you feel? That is easy. Can you also imagine what would happen if you did that in return?

How about the children? When I tell parents their children will listen to them when, and only when, they have been listened to, the reaction is usually one of resentment. Parents seem to feel that children are supposed to listen to them simply because they are the parent, and that is how it should be. What would happen if you really concentrated on what is in your child's bucket?

The magic of the bucket works in the office with coworkers and bosses. It works anywhere people contact people.

I made a sales call on an important company I was hoping to do business with. The night before the meeting, I laid plans to concentrate on their buckets instead of my own needs and desires. I determined to be impressed by them instead of trying to be impressive to them. It did not take long for the magic to work. After a time of exploring who they were and what they needed, the head of the company said, "Please tell us everything about you and your company."

Since I make my living making speeches, I have studied the art of public speaking most of my life. The times when I am successful are the times when my concentration is on what the audience needs and how my presentation fits that need. When I go in there to "Wow" them, I miss. When I go in there to get in their buckets, I hit.

While you have your buckets out, maybe we could think through some other places these keys could be used and the principles applied. Where do you need to use these? Who are you having a struggle communicating with right now? You are the only one who can answer that, but maybe some suggestions will stir up your thinking.

This might be a good time to write out your thoughts and plans for getting into the buckets of the people you are working with—clients, patients, families, church members—whoever comes to you with a bucket. A good place to start would be to write out what you think they must be feeling.

_____

_____

_____

_____

_____

_____

_____

Notes

The Power Of Presence

I have told this story many times, but nothing captures the essence of presence like Mr. Lockstone. If you've heard it before, please read it again in the context of our discussion.

When I was a very young minister, I received an urgent call one morning. There had been a SIDS death. A mother found her young son dead in the crib, and she had rushed to her mother's house with the body. I walked into utter chaos. Several neighbor women had also gathered and were physically restraining the young mother while trying to keep her from touching the body of her son. This was in the '50s, and that was how things were done in those days. When I walked in, they said, "You must help us; she should not touch the body. She must give it up." I had no idea whether she should or not, but as I took a step toward the group, someone said, "Mr. Lockstone is here." Mr. Lockstone was the funeral director in our town. If I could bottle the feeling that swept that room and sell it, I would die a very wealthy man. All of a sudden we felt, "It will be all right. He will know what to do. We are not alone."

Mr. Lockstone waved his hand, and the women knew that they were to leave the room. He looked at me, and I knew I was supposed to stay. I have no idea how we all knew that from a wave and a look, but we knew and followed his directions. He took the young mother by the hand and led her to the couch. He placed the body of her son in her arms and spoke the only words he said all morning. He said, "Now you hold your boy as long as you want to, and when you are finished, I will take care of things." She rocked her boy for a while and then handed his body to Mr. Lockstone and said, "Will you take care of him for me?"

Mr. Lockstone did not speak. He simply nodded and took the baby into his arms. I stood there in amazement. I was witnessing the power of presence. His being there was all that mattered.

All of us have experienced those kinds of encounters, when we were in deep need, and someone came to be with us. My wife had emergency bypass surgery while we were on a trip 300 miles from home. That afternoon three friends walked into the waiting room. They had driven there to be with me. They did not say anything. They did not have to. They gave me the gift of presence.

It may sound ludicrous, but that is how people feel when you arrive. You do not come bringing great truths nor wonderfully worded messages. You come bringing presence. When someone hurts and you bring that, they are helped.

We had a grandson who was born on Christmas Eve and died on Christmas Day. He only lived thirty-four hours. Before he died, the doctor unplugged the tubes and machines and brought him to us. We held him and bonded with him until death came. As soon as he was gone, we had a very strange experience. The other grandfather present was a minister. The father was a minister. I served as a minister for thirty-seven years and have spoken about death and dying for years. Still, not a person in that room knew what to do next. We sat there in stunned silence with no ideas at all. Then the funeral director walked in. The same feeling swept the room that I had felt all those years ago after the SIDS death. "It's going to be all right. He will know what to do. We are not alone."

That is the power of presence. This is not rocket science, nor is it something only certain people have. This is not some gift only the gifted bring. Anyone who learns to listen brings the power of presence wherever they go and, if you are one of those, when you walk in, those same feelings sweep the room...*We are not alone.*

We have looked at the principles of care through presence. Now let's look into the buckets of people facing some of the major struggles in life.

Notes

_____
_____
_____
_____
_____
_____
_____
_____
_____
_____
_____
_____
_____
_____
_____
_____
_____
_____
_____
_____
_____
_____
_____

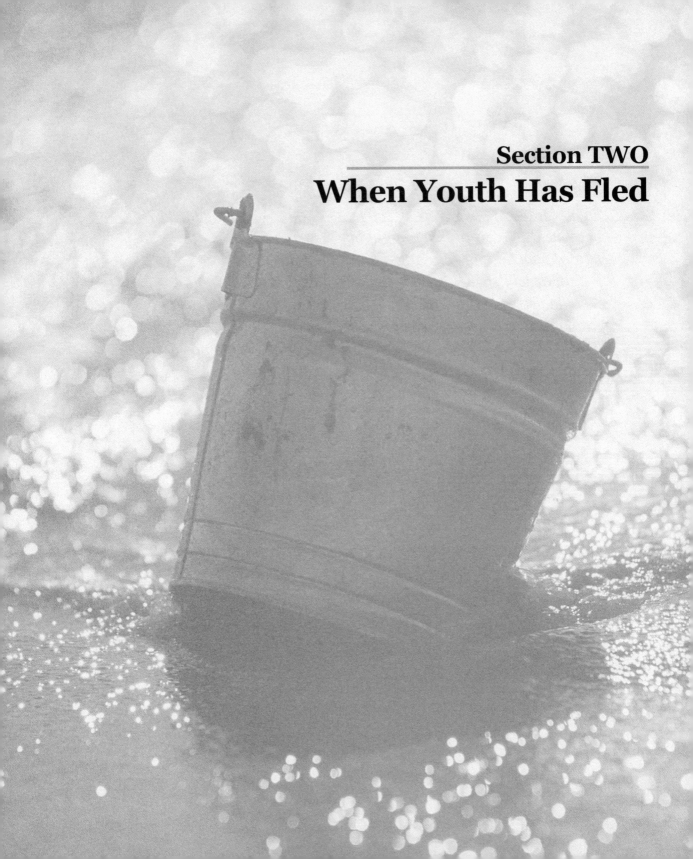

Section TWO
When Youth Has Fled

*Being aware of your own fears about dying will help you
immeasurably to be aware of the fears of the aging person. Just
imagine deeply what those might be:
fear of pain, fear of suffering, fear of indignity,
fear of dependence, fear that lives we have led have been
meaningless, fear of separation, fear of losing control, fear of
losing respect. Perhaps our greatest fear
of all is fear of fear itself, which grows more and more powerful
the more we evade it.*

–Sogyal Rinpoche
The Tibetan Book of Living and Dying

When Youth Has Fled

They may smile and seem sweet, but some of the loneliest people are the aged, particularly those whose health has forced them to leave their homes and live with one of their children or in a care facility. What do you suppose is in their buckets? It seems strange to me that there are very few articles or books written about what that must feel like. After years of trying to look into some buckets, and after growing old enough to know what is facing me, may I share some feelings and issues I find there?

Suddenly Old

None of us know we are old. I have asked many elderly people what it feels like to be old. I have never had an answer. None of them knew they were. Everyone thinks he is about twenty years younger than he is. This is true because it still feels the same. Your joints may ache more, and your mind is slower to remember, but it does not feel like you think old would feel. My father used to say he was going to the nursing home to visit the old people. He was eighty-five at the time. There were only two people there who were older than he was, but he didn't know that. He had no idea he was old. None of us do.

Then, we are suddenly old. Our health breaks, or it breaks far enough that we cannot ignore it any longer. Great changes are forced upon us. We begin to lose control. That may be the hardest part of the whole deal. We begin to resent our children because they seem to be taking over our lives. They begin to make decisions about us instead of with us. Often the issue is not where we will live so much as who makes that decision.

Think of the house where your parents live. They may have been there for many years. They know every board in it. They have treasures there that you will not be able to give away at a rummage sale, but they are treasures to them. Suddenly, the family must step in and tell them they cannot live there anymore. This is often caused by the death of a spouse. The aged loved one is facing the loss of a mate and, before she can grieve that loss, she must face other losses.

They will lose most of their stuff. Things they have enjoyed and even treasured must be sacrificed to the lack of space in the new living arrangement. It is an arrangement, not a home, to them.

They will lose their social life, their sense of independence, their freedom of movement, spontaneity and the comfort of the old neighborhood. One great loss will be the family traditions, those things they always did at Christmas, Hanukkah, Memorial Day or any of the other holidays. We take those things for granted, but they become dear when they are gone.

They want to talk about these losses, but no one will listen. They don't know how to say it, so they may just say they want to go home or that they miss their home. The family will usually do almost anything to change the subject. The prevailing idea is that the more they talk about it, the more they will miss it, so the subject is changed and some positive prattle is thrown at them. "Oh! You will love your new place. They have Bingo every Thursday night." The loved one just shuts up and retreats into a closed and lonely world.

Some react with demands and noise. They become the problem children of the nursing facility. Nothing is any good. Quite often they are fine until their families come to see them, and then it is time for a pity party or an explosion. A lot of times, this is nothing more than the reaction of a lonely person whom no one will hear.

Others hide it behind a smile and fake happiness, but there is a growing sense of melancholy about them.

After a conference in Pennsylvania where I spoke on this subject, a man talked to me about his father. He said, "My father had to sell his farm in Indiana and move here with us. He was born on that farm and so was his father. He wants to talk about the farm all of the time, but I have been afraid to let him do so. Won't talking about it make him miss it more? You seemed to say that he needs to talk. Is that really what you are saying?" I said, "If necessary, I will get on both knees and beg you to let him talk."

Get into that man's bucket for a few moments. What would it feel like to lose the farm where both you and your father were born? What would it feel like to have that loss ignored and trivialized with changed subjects and "look on the positive side" babble?

My mother had to go to a nursing home for three months with a broken hip. She knew she would only be there for three months, and she knew it was necessary for her to be there. She laid guilt on me every time I went to visit her. She did not want to jump on me, so she would tell me how bad things were at the facility. Complaints about the food, the care, and the temperature in the place flowed in a constant stream at every visit.

I would respond to her complaints with, "Now, Mother you know…" We should get that phrase out of our vocabularies. It means "Get ready, Mom, I am about to trivialize you." I would say, "Now, Mother you know you are only here for three months," or "The doctor said you had to be here," or, "You know this is the finest nursing home in the whole area." I woke up one night listening to my own speeches. In spite of all the talking I had done about listening, I was not practicing it with my own mother.

The next day when she registered her complaint, I pulled my chair up close and said, "You are angry about being in here aren't you?" She responded with, "Yes, and I am so ashamed of myself. I know I am only here for three months and that I need to be here. I should be bigger than this. Every day when you leave, I promise myself not to do that anymore, but when you come in, it just comes out." I said, "It is all right to be angry. If I have to live here, I am going to be angry. It is all right to tell me you are angry. I will understand." From that day until the day she died, I gave her the gift of anger. We do that when we get into their buckets and simply understand.

I once asked a man who knew he was dying what
he needed above all in those who were caring for him. He said, "For
someone to look as if they are trying to understand me." Indeed it is
impossible to understand fully another person, but I never forgot
that he did not ask for success but only that someone should
care enough to try.

–Cicely Saunders
Founder of the British Hospice movement

Notes

_____

_____

_____

_____

_____

_____

_____

_____

_____

_____

_____

_____

_____

_____

_____

_____

_____

_____

_____

_____

_____

_____

_____

Section THREE

When Care Must Be Given

After five years my mother still recognized us,
but the dullness in her eyes, her loss of appetite and her
inability to enjoy anything... fashioned a trap
she could not even comprehend.
Captive to a fragmented mind and an increasingly frail body,
she was constantly restless, jumping up randomly and heading
for the nearest door as if trying to outrun some demon force...
My once-elegant mother would have been appalled
to see herself—one of a dozen ill-clad denizens in the dining
room of an assisted-living wing—and me, the dutiful daughter,
trying to coax her into one more spoonful of applesauce.
Her inability to name it, my inability to change it, became a
strip of frustration, a tandem curse.

–Nancy Cobb
In Lieu of Flowers
A Conversation for the Living

When Care Must Be Given

The other side of the fence is no picnic either. What do you think it feels like to suddenly face the long term care of a loved one? A spouse that now demands more care than can be provided in the home. A parent that can no longer stay at home and you cannot care for him in yours. Suddenly you are faced with making decisions you never dreamed you would have to make.

I promised my parents and my wife's parents they would never live in a nursing home. My mother-in-law, my father, and my mother all died in care facilities. May I tell you about those kinds of buckets?

You wonder if you have failed to love them or if you even know how to love at all. Other people have taken care of their loved ones all the way to the end. Why are you not strong enough or loving enough to do that for yours? There is no way to understand that life has made some major changes in this area. Loved ones now live longer, and, in that process, they can demand more care than ever before. I now know that I made a promise to my loved ones, and I kept the promise. They just outlived the promise. The fact is we are now living beyond our children's ability to care for us. However, it does not feel that way when you are the one telling your father he must live in a nursing home.

You feel a great deal of confusion and fear. A great deal of the stress comes from the fact that we do not know how we are supposed to feel about the loved one. Since he is a spouse or a parent, we know we are supposed to love him no matter what the circumstances. No one tells us that even though we love him, we will still get tired. We will still get angry. We will still feel burdened and guilty because we do. There is no way to know that our expectations are far too high to ever be reached.

I call that not knowing what is "normal." If we cannot accept these feelings as the normal reaction to the circumstances we face, we will fill our buckets with not only guilt but stresses that can do great damage to us.

If these reach extremes, and they often do, then people can become obsessed with care. Often, they cannot stand how they feel inside, so they overcompensate by trying to make everything perfect on the outside. They can become a nursing home's nightmare. Nothing is right. They can drive their families to distraction with their constant barrage of needs and complaints. No one wants to be around them, much less let them talk through the feelings that are driving them.

Often, people feel guilty—horribly guilty. As a matter of fact, guilt becomes the major problem to be faced. Some will feel more guilt than others because they have spent their lives trying to earn the love of their parents, and now they must give tough love in an area that displeases the very folks they have spent their lives trying to please.

Far too often these decisions are made without much help from family or siblings. Too many families hang the care on one person and then feel free to criticize every decision that person makes.

I will never forget the very harried woman who had total responsibility for her mother. She had a sister in the same city, who gave no help at all. The sister was wealthy and did not work outside of the home. This lady had a full time job and gave the care. Her sister did not even help financially. Work demands forced the lady to ask for some help. Her sister agreed to take the mother for two weeks. After one week, she called and demanded that the woman come after the mother. When she arrived, the sister met her on the porch and said, "Don't you dare put my mother in a nursing home."

Consider the woman who cared for her mother and listened to her brothers complain about her decisions but never offered to help in any way. The brothers then sued her over how she spent the money for the care.

These, and many other stories, made me add this chapter to this book. If you want to spend some time giving care that no one else is giving, find some long-term caregivers and get into their buckets.

It may take more than one effort to get into these buckets. Most are so overwhelmed with giving care, they have no idea that they need care for themselves. They will spend the time relating story after story about the experience of caring, but rarely will they tell how it is affecting them or their lives. I asked an Alzheimer's support group what *they* had lost. It took several minutes and several tries to get a response. They were so accustomed to talking about the disease and the patient, that they had no ready answer for my question.

Finally, they began to tell of lost social lives, of lost time for themselves, of lost communication, of lost companionship, of lost intimacy, of lost spontaneity, and of lost history. We were all amazed at the list and even more amazed at the fact that not one person in the room had ever spoken of those losses, and no one had a person who he thought would be interested enough to hear about his losses.

Helping long-term caregivers is not as dramatic or exciting as some other areas, but there are no areas of greater need and none with as little being done to meet the need.

Like end-of-life midwives, they guided us with veteran skill,
anticipating our needs, asking the right questions,
advancing and retreating with delicacy and respect.
I watched them counsel other families and care for
one another as well. The collaborative nature of this work
gave one the instant feeling of belonging.

–Nancy Cobb
In Lieu of Flowers
A Conversation for the Living

Notes

Section FOUR

When Death Draws Near

Our instinct for survival is so strong, so deep-seated,
that we defend ourselves against death by denying it.
If we bring it to the surface in conversation with friends or loved
ones, we're called morbid, depressing… and when our elderly
parents or grandparents try to bring our attention to their fears,
plans or desires concerning their deaths, we tend to brush them
off by saying, "Oh come on, don't be so gloomy. You know
you're going to outlive all of us." Or we make a joke like, "Oh,
Grandma, you're too mean to die." Or we say, "Not in front of
the children, Dad. We'll talk about it later."
Discussing death is a "no-no" in our culture.

–Kay Kramer
Conversations at Midnight

When Death Draws Near

The first time I ever let someone talk to me about her dying, I had to hold the chair with both hands to keep myself from running from the room. I was not raised in that kind of intimacy, and talking to someone about her death is the ultimate intimacy. My usual response when someone brought up the subject was to throw some scripture or prayer at him and get out of the room. If the person said he did not think he was going to make it, which is the classic opening for a conversation, I would say, "Oh! Yes you are. You are looking much better." My mode of operation was to lie and get out of the room. One morning a woman broached the subject, and I asked if she wanted to talk about it. She said she did, and I held the chair until my knuckles turned white.

I was no different than most people. We do not "do death" well. Most of us can't stand to be around it. Most of us can't stand to think about death, much less talk about it. George Carlin says it will not be long before we will call death a "terminal incident."

I suppose there is a positive side to our fear. The renewed interest in health may be the result of our efforts to live forever. We seem to love talking about health more than we enjoy exercising and dieting, but at least the subject is on the table. That may be the good side of our fear, but the bad side more than offsets any good.

Fear Of Death Costs Us Dying Ritual

A physician at a conference said, "No one dies of old age anymore." I asked him what he meant and he said, "Old age is no longer considered a cause of death. You cannot write that on a death certificate. People must die of some illness with a long name and after a lengthy struggle. Often, the struggle is made even longer because we see death as a defeat."

This fear not only means we make death a long struggle, it also robs us of the rituals that help us through the dying process. I call that dying ritual. My grandfather had dying ritual. He died many years before modern medicine and modern fears of death. A spider bit him and he developed blood poisoning, which was a death sentence in those days. He knew he was going to die and so did the family. No one tried to deny the facts nor hide them from him. He had the chance to call each of his children to his bedside for a last private talk. They never forgot that experience.

Most likely that could not happen now. We have an almost instinctive fear or superstition about letting people know they are going to die. Somehow we have developed the notion that as soon as they know, they will give up all hope and die. We seem to think there is no way they can continue to live another day after learning about their condition. We hide the truth from the dying. We do so even when it is evident they already know.

There is no sense in even trying to decide whether someone should be told the truth or not. They already know. There are too many clues and too much whispering in the halls for them to not know. Their body tells them the truth even if doctors and families refuse to do so.

We tend to put the dying in isolated situations. Family visits are restricted and nursing staffs use bustle and professional appearance to keep an arm's length away from dealing with the fact of death.

Fear costs us healing rituals. The modern day funeral is sanitized to hide the fact that someone has died. More and more families are choosing to have some very nonthreatening memorial service after the body has been buried or cremated. We seem to be as afraid of tears as we are of death.

Since that first scary day when the woman said she wanted to talk about her dying and I clung to the chair, some of the most meaningful experiences of my life have happened in those kinds of settings.

A nursing home administrator asked me to talk with one of his patients. She was hysterical, and he was in panic. The woman had a problem with her throat and could not speak. I had never met her, and she had no idea who I was, so we had to spend a great deal of time trying to establish communication. Since she had to write her thoughts on a child's magic slate, this took all morning. When we finally began to talk freely, I asked her what she was afraid of. She immediately wrote "DEATH." I caught myself before I began a long dissertation on death and the hereafter, and said, "Are you afraid of death, or are you afraid of dying?" She gradually revealed that she was afraid of choking to death. I asked her if she wanted me to find out how she was going to die. She indicated that she did. I asked her if she wanted me to tell her the truth, no matter what I found, and she was very sure in her "yes" response.

I finally persuaded her physician to tell me how she was going to die. That took some real effort on my part. It was hard for him to even acknowledge that she might die. His whole world seemed to hang on the idea that none of his patients ever died. He said she would choke, but she would be in a coma long before her death and would not be aware of any choking. I told her and kept up with her for the two years she had left. She was never again in panic. Since we had broken the barrier to talking about death, she felt free to talk with me openly and often. We even were able to joke about it, and it seemed to make her passage a natural and peaceful movement from one life to another.

Another woman chose me as the person she wanted to talk with about her dying. I think people often make a choice in this area. It may be that we need to learn how to allow them to choose. We cannot assume we are the one to do this. They have the right, and that right should be honored.

The problem was with the family. They were afraid to allow "the talk" to happen. It was evident that they felt if the talk happened, she would die. She would send for me, but they would not allow me to see her in private. They would stand guard beside her bed for the duration of my visits. I talked with them in private and explained what she wanted to do, and they would promise privacy for my next visit, but they could not allow it.

One day in the hospital room, her husband was talking with someone else across the room. She drew me close and said, "Doug, I am just so tired." I said, "Are you saying you want to go on?" She would not answer that. She said, "Well, I have those grandchildren." She had raised her grandchildren who were now young adults and out of the home. I said, "Yes, and you did a great job raising them. They will be fine. If you want to go on it's all right." She pulled me down and kissed me. In thirty minutes she was gone. She just needed permission.

These experiences have left me with some observations that I think are valid. The first one has already been established: people want to talk about their dying. If ever there was a need to establish the significance of what is happening to us, it must be when we are facing death. If ever there was a time when that is almost impossible, it is when we are facing death. No one wants to hear us.

The second observation is that the dying will choose the person or persons they wish to talk to. Quite often they will not choose a family member. Family members are too close to take a chance with. What if they did not want to talk? Family members are the least likely to be the ones who are willing to face the death, much less talk. Usually the person will look outside the immediate family. We cannot make the choice for them, nor can we designate ourselves as the chosen one. We can let them know we are willing, but we cannot force them to talk nor force them to talk to us.

The third observation is that no one knows how to broach the subject. Most of the time the dying will almost talk in code, sending out little hints that we must be carefully focused to pick up. They are not going to say, "I am dying, and I want to talk with you about that." They will more likely say, "I don't think I am going to make it," or, "I don't know what is going on," or, like the woman in my story, "I am just so tired." An elderly person saying, "I don't know why God doesn't take me," may be an open invitation to this kind of conversation.

The need to talk is the genius of hospice. Hospice in America started out as a group of volunteers who decided to become comfortable enough with death and dying to sit with folks while death came. A great deal of their training and emphasis was not only on allowing people to die in peace, it was also in providing someone for them to talk with about their deaths. They also emphasized having someone for the family to talk with about the impending death.

The need for presence is seen very dramatically in the story of the crucifixion of Jesus. Apart from any religious connotation, here is an example of a man who wanted to talk with someone while he was dying, and there was no one to talk with. He wanted to talk about how he felt about the people who killed him. There was no one there, so he said, "Forgive them, they don't have any idea what they are doing." He wanted to talk about his mother. There was no one, so he asked a friend to take care of her. He wanted someone to know about how it all felt. All he could do was speak to the wind that he was thirsty. He wanted to talk about how lonely it was. All he could do was shout to the heavens that it felt as if God had forsaken him. He needed permission to die, and there was no one there, so he just told anyone that could hear that it was over.

The problem is, we still let people die like that, alone with no one to talk to. In our efforts to protect them or to keep them alive, we let them die in loneliness and fear. The best way for us to understand this is to, once again, use the bucket idea.

If you were dying, what would be in your bucket? What would you be feeling? What would you be thinking? Let's say you are in a hospital, and it is evident to you that your illness is terminal. No one tells you that is so. Your family carries on with forced happiness that you see through, but you do not feel free to expose their charade. First, you don't know how uncomfortable that would make them, and second, you have no idea how you would react either. Friends come to call, and they, too, have that "too cheery for words" look plastered on their faces. The medical staff seem to hide it as they go about their business and then get out of your room as fast as possible. You figure it all out. You are dying. What now?

Would you want to talk?

_____

_____

_____

What would you want to talk about?

_____

_____

_____

_____

_____

_____

_____

_____

_____

_____

Would you feel the need to establish the significance of what is happening to you?

_____

_____

_____

_____

_____

_____

_____

_____

Please take a moment and write all of this down. Try to feel it until it becomes almost real to you.

Now let's say I am one of your loved ones, and I come to see you. What is in my bucket?

_____

_____

_____

_____

_____

_____

_____

_____

_____

_____

Would I be scared that you will want to talk about dying?

_____

_____

_____

_____

_____

_____

_____

_____

Would I be at a total loss as to what to say?

_____

_____

_____

_____

_____

_____

_____

_____

_____

Would I feel an intense need to cheer you up?

_____

_____

_____

_____

_____

_____

_____

_____

_____

I visit and avoid your bucket while you avoid mine.
How does that make you feel?

_____

_____

_____

_____

_____

_____

_____

What does that add to your pain?

_____

_____

_____

_____

_____

_____

_____

_____

_____

_____

_____

Let's say I am a clergy person. I come to see you. My bucket is full of all kinds of wonderful stuff. I know all about God and Heaven. I also have some dilemmas in my bucket. On the one hand, I want to tell you about life beyond life in whatever terms that are true to my faith. On the other hand, I feel tremendous pressure to cheer you up and give you hope for getting better, so I pray for you to get well.

How does that make you feel?

_____

_____

_____

_____

_____

_____

Are you more lonely than ever?

_____

_____

_____

_____

_____

_____

_____

_____

_____

_____

This has great meaning to me because I saw it happen with my Uncle Joe. Joe was the one kinsman I was closest to and my favorite. He was my mother's brother, but he was only nine years older than me. I had looked up to him all of my life. He retired early and spent several years driving me to speaking engagements whenever possible. We had wonderful times teasing each other and talking about life its own self.

Joe had a heart attack and then had another during a test in the hospital. His kidneys shut down and refused to start again. The doctors told the family that there was no hope. The family asked the doctors to tell him, but they failed to do so. I arrived the next day, which was a Saturday, so the doctor would not be back until Monday. I spent the day watching the process of denial. The family would go in at the appointed times and act like all was well. They approached each visit with great fear. They were petrified at the thought of Joe asking them for the truth. No one wanted to be the one to tell him.

Late that evening, he asked me. My insides shook, and my knees knocked while I told him the truth. I had been in this kind of place many times but not with someone so close and someone I loved so dearly. He was relieved. He already knew, and now we could stop acting. I brought the family in and could not help but realize that I had given Joe the same kind of dying ritual his father, my grandfather, had many years ago. He had the chance to tell each of his children and grandchildren how much he loved them. They had the chance to tell him as well. His wife, his brother, and I all had experiences with Joe that night that we will treasure all of our lives.

Joe made the decision to unplug the machines and move into hospice care. He lived less than a week, but it was a week of sharing and caring with his family and friends. No one felt the need to act like Joe wasn't dying. My Uncle Joe did not die lonely. He did not do so because a long time before that day I held on to a chair and learned how to listen to people talk about their dying.

That is the power of presence.

Without perhaps realizing it, we had committed one of the worst of errors that can be made during terminal illness. We had decided incorrectly, and in opposition to every principle of our lives together, that it was more important to protect one another from the open admission of a painful truth than it was to achieve a final sharing that might have snatched an enduring comfort and even some dignity from the anguishing fact of death. We denied ourselves what should have been ours.

–Sherwin Nuland
How We Die

Notes

Section FIVE
When Grief Overwhelms

People who would comfort us could not know that no one in mourning will respond to cautious invitation.
Mourners need the brave souls who dare to hold them, touch them, to stay rather than leave when the tears begin to flow.
They do not need sage advice or perfect words.
Simple human touch is the mourner's balm.

–Barbara Lazear Ascher
Landscape Without Gravity

When Grief Overwhelms

Time does not heal all wounds. All time does is allow wounds to fester and create more and more hurt. Too often grief is seen as a period of sadness that will pass in time. That has been the prevailing concept, but the more we study the consequences of unresolved grief, the more we realize the prevailing concept was wrong. I think grief is one of the major social problems of our time. That sounds rather dramatic, but we have no idea how many of the things we call social problems had their beginning in grief that was not properly dealt with and was allowed to fester until it came out in some other problem.

We have no idea how much divorce comes from grief. There is no way to establish this statistically because the impact may not show up for many years. When it does, we rarely connect the divorce with the long ago grieving experience. Grief places burdens on any relationship. The needs are so great and the expectations so high that wedges can be driven into the marriage. These wedges can certainly be overcome, but they also can be ignored and, ultimately, split a couple apart.

A woman said, "I am not surprised to hear that grief can cause marital difficulties because it happened to me. It took thirty years, but my marriage began to suffer the night my son was killed."

Grief can be the cause of substance abuse. A beautiful and talented young woman was murdered. She was in the wrong place at the wrong time and was killed in a drug deal. Everyone was shocked that she, of all people, would have a substance problem. No one made the connection to the fact that her father was killed when she was nine years of age. Even though her father died in the early '80s, there was very little help available for those in grief. Time was supposed to heal the wound. Her difficulties with life can be traced to that death and her efforts to just "buck up" and get over it.

Lenore Terr's book, *Too Scared To Cry,* is an account of the students in Chowchilla, California, who were captured and placed in an old truck trailer buried in the earth. They were able to dig themselves out, and no one was hurt, so no one dealt with the trauma of this event. Dr. Terr's study picks them up about six years later. The high rates of early marriage, pregnancy without marriage, and substance abuse are more than proof that grief or trauma unresolved can have a devastating impact on the future of those involved. Learning to listen to those in grief is a far more important step than most people can ever know.

A woman recently gave me a wonderful description of the walk through grief. She pointed to her left shoulder and said:

> My daughter sits on my shoulder. She died four years ago, and now she lives in my heart, but I sense her presence there on my shoulder. I talk to her often. I know she is there, whether I am talking to her or not. Having her there is certainly not what I want nor can it ever replace her being alive and with me in the flesh, but it is better than it was at first. For the first two or three years, she was right here.

With that she held her hand right in front of her face.

> Every thought I had was about her. I saw life through her. I stopped being me and became her bereaved mother. Her death took over my entire life. All I could think about was that she was gone. When someone would ask me how I was doing, I would want to scream, "Can't you see? She is right there in front of my face. How dare you ask?"

The move from in front of my face to my shoulder was long and hard. I call it "moving from face-to-face to heart-to-heart," but don't let that sweet saying fool you. It was brutal. I fought the move. Every time she would start to move, I would pull her back. I was afraid that moving meant forgetting. Maybe it meant I was not going to love her properly or think of her often enough. I felt the need to prove that I would never forget her, as if I ever could. I seemed to have some great need to honor her and to be sure others did the same. When members of my family seemed to be moving on, I would seethe inside. How dare they forget her? How dare they not keep her right in front of their faces just like I was?

The day finally came, and I was able to let her begin to move. It was scary. I felt an even greater loss and seemed to go through a period of renewed and even deeper grief. I slowly surrendered, and she moved to my heart.

I like having her there. I think she even likes it better there. She would not want to dominate my life forever. The strange thing is, I feel closer to her now than before. Even though she was right in front of my face, all I could do then was feel the pain of her passing and cry. Now I can talk to her, and, though you may think I am crazy, I think she hears, and I feel a response.

Grief is the natural response to any loss. There is a built-in process that I call nature's way of healing a broken heart. When I first began to write about grief, I presented it in "stages." Almost all of the early authors did the same. Even then I did not like the idea of stages. Stages imply clear-cut lines of demarcation, and grief is rarely that clear-cut. People flip-flop through periods of change. They can be in two stages at the same time. This has led me to look for other analogies to use. A friend of mine, Paula Loring, says, "Grief is when the heart breaks, when the heart bleeds, when the heart surrenders, and when the heart heals." I love the mental picture her definition presents.

My favorite analogy is that grief is like peeling an onion—it comes off one layer at a time, and you cry a lot. One reason I like that analogy is that it allows me to show that grief is as unique as a fingerprint, and everyone grieves in his own way. If I handed an onion to each person in an audience, no two onions would be the same, and every one would peel his onion in his own way. Some would peel fast, some slow, some would play with the little roots on the bottom, others with the peak at the top, but each person would have a unique onion and peel it in a unique way. That is grief.

Having an analogy is a great tool for us to use when speaking about grief. However, for our purposes here, analogies do not help much. Our goal with this course is to understand the listening process as it relates to grieving people. The onion analogy does allow us to explore the differences in some of the grieving situations we will face.

The problem with stages and analogies is we tend to lump all grieving into one pattern. It is true that grieving seems to loosely follow a pattern, but the person in grief does not see it that way, and being told he is just like everyone else tends to trivialize his grief.

Our company produced a video of a mother whose daughter died by suicide. We prepared for that video by spending a day brainstorming together. She repeated over and over, "If you have not walked the walk, you cannot understand." When we asked her to describe the grief after suicide, she used the same language that any other bereaved mother would use. Her video does not say anything that is unique to the grieving process. Same language, same experiences, but to her, they are totally different. After the taping, we talked about this and came to the conclusion that the differences are in perception and heightened dimensions in certain types of death. These dimensions are present in all grief, but they are stronger and more prevalent in some cases. Some examples follow:

Death of a Child

The death of a child has a heightened need for significance. A young mother, whose husband died quite early, remarried and then suffered the death of a child, explained the differences between those two experiences. She said there was no way for her to differentiate between the pain, but the grief following the death of her mate was a process of turning loose, of saying good-bye. The grief following the death of her child was a process of holding on, of trying not to say good-bye. She said, "You don't feel like the child lived long enough to establish her significance, and you need to establish it for her." As you will see, the need for significance is prevalent in all grief. The need is just greater here. That is why a person whose child has died will almost hug you if you will call the child's name. They want the child remembered.

Stillbirths

A stillbirth has a lonely dimension. The mother is the only one who knew the child. The father may have felt the baby kick or seen an ultrasound, but that mother bonded with the child at conception. She now must explain the significance of a life to a world that considers stillbirth a minor grief.

Suicide

Suicide has a shattered dimension. It is almost as if the onion has been torn apart, and people need to put it back together before they can grieve. I watched a couple spend at least a year in research after their 14-year-old son hanged himself. They had to know everything that could have possibly caused him to take his life. They never found out, of course, but they could not get on with their grieving until the onion was back together.

Murder

Murder has a delayed dimension. Everything is on hold until the murderer is caught. Then it is on hold until the trial. The tendency is to think these will be magic days. People believe they will feel differently afterwards. I am companioning a mother whose daughter was murdered. It took two years for the trial to happen. We made some progress in that time, but waiting for the trial dominated her thinking. Then came the trial. No one could ever imagine what a victim's family experiences in a trial. The victim has no rights at all. My friend felt like the whole process focused on proving that the murderer was the one to feel sorry for and protect. In the process of protecting him, her daughter's value was lost. The trial is over, and her grieving is almost back to the beginning.

If there are no set patterns for us to use in guiding people through this experience, and if they perceive their grief in ways unique unto themselves, then all that is left for us to do is simply listen. It is time to get the buckets out again and discover that instead of trying to pour the things in our bucket into theirs, we need to get into their bucket with them. That is scary. We have no idea what they are going to say or ask. We have no idea how much control they can maintain. There will always be the fear of saying the wrong things. But, if we are going to help, we must get into their pain with them. When we get into their buckets, we allow them to discover some wonderfully healing gifts.

Safety

If you boil down everything all of the grief authors have ever written or said, it comes down to "permission." People need permission to grieve. My involvement in studying grief started when a young mother said, after her child died, "Don't take my grief away from me." I realized that I had spent my life trying to do just that. Instead of hurting along side, I was standing off pouring platitudes out of my own bucket because of my own fear.

Permission demands safe places and safe people. Safe people are those who are comfortable with whatever direction the grieving process goes.

They don't feel like they must "fix" it. The people who help the most are not the ones with all of the answers but rather those who are comfortable with no answers. Those are the people who give permission.

The Right To Be Angry

Very few grieving people will admit to being angry. Most of them will not recognize that they are. The anger caused by grief comes across as hurt or frustration. Whether it is recognized or not, anger is almost a given. Anger is the natural reaction to hurt, so there will be some anger. The anger is healthy. I think anger is the force that drives us toward learning to cope. We seem to hit bottom, get mad, and start clawing our way back out of the pit.

While anger is healthy, people still need to deal with it. Anger left to itself may well result in depression, so it needs to be handled. Sometimes doing physical things helps. I met a woman who buys cheap dishes at garage sales, and when she feels the need, breaks them into the garbage can.

The problem with anger is that it does not float well. We need to be angry *at* something. Anger has a way of focusing. Where it focuses matters. There are some places where anger tends to focus that sound bad but are really quite healthy.

Some people get angry with God. That scares the clergy, but it is not a bad place for anger to focus. Almost every expression of God I know presents a God big enough to take our anger. The fear is that people will not get over it, and they will be mad at God for the rest of their lives. Grief is a transition. Where they are today is not where they will be tomorrow. The ones who never get over the anger toward God are usually the ones that were criticized for the way they felt. They built up defenses and then must defend their defenses.

Anger may also focus on physicians, ministers, hospitals, even funeral directors. All of these are uncomfortable but not bad places for anger to focus. Anger may settle on a mate. This is the major cause of the marital strain that often comes with a death. Even that is not an unhealthy place for anger.

If someone is angry, remember the nursery rhyme "leave them alone and they will come home wagging their tails behind them." This, too, shall pass.

The one place we do not want anger to focus is internally. We do not want people to turn the anger on themselves. You will recognize this because the person will begin to obsessively play the game of "if only." Everyone plays some of that game, but these folks will be obsessive about it. They will build elaborate scaffolds to support a case against themselves. I remember a mother whose daughter-in-law was murdered saying, "I was with the kids when they were looking for an apartment. I found that one and took them to see it. If I had not found that apartment, they would not have been in that apartment; the killer would not have found her there, so her death is my fault."

We do not change the focus of anger by trying to change the focus of anger. As they talk and we listen without comment, they will gradually gain insight enough to see through their anger, even though they may not know it is anger. As anger is expressed, it tends to peak and subside. They will gradually talk it through and refocus.

I remember a couple, whose daughter died by suicide spending a solid hour criticizing their church, pastor, and friends over how little help they received. After about an hour, they seemed to run out of steam. If you remember our talk about timing in a previous chapter, then you know that the time for me to talk was after their anger peaked. I said, "May I tell you what I am hearing you say?" They gave permission and

I said, "What I am hearing is that you are angry. You should be angry." I am no miracle worker, but their anger refocused at that moment. Suddenly, they were dealing with the anger. The man began to express how angry he really was. The wife said, "You know why I am so angry with all of those friends? I don't want to be angry with my daughter."

Listening To The Cry For Significance

The most important word in grieving is "significance." It becomes the major drive in the lives of those in grief. The woman I am companioning said after attending the trial of the person who killed her daughter:

> When I first started coming here, you talked about significance, and I saw a little bit of the meaning, but every day I see that it really is what I am trying to do. The whole trial hurt because it was about the guy who killed my daughter, and no one saw how significant she was. The defense tried to make everyone feel sorry for the guy, but no one stood up for my daughter. That hurt most of all.

Establish the Significance of the Loss

When a death happens, there is a need to establish significance on at least three levels. For this discussion, let's consider a woman who has lost her husband. Maybe we need to get the buckets out again.

Can you imagine what is in the woman's bucket? One would assume that her main concern would be what happens to her husband after death, but usually that will not be the case. The first issue on the list of normal needs is survival. She wants people to look at what is happening to *her*. She wants to know if she can survive this pain. She is not being selfish; she is just trying to survive.

In most cases, that is not what people talk to her about. Usually, they will focus on her husband being in a better place and not having to suffer anymore. Or, they will tell her how fortunate she is to have had such a fine man and good marriage. When that happens, she must feel like they are talking in some unknown language.

The first thing she must do is figure out for herself what she has lost. It is almost as if she has to inventory the loss before she can grieve it. We have no idea what we have lost until it is gone. My wife had serious surgery, and I thought she was going to die. I had loved her for many years, but I discovered value in her that day that I never knew existed. I still don't know what she is worth, and I won't unless she dies first. Then, and only then, will I begin to know.

Every day this woman will think of something else he did, or something else he said, or something else she liked about him, or something else she wanted to ask him, or something else she wanted to do with him. It is inventory time, and she needs someone in the bucket with her.

Most of the efforts at comfort will be contrary to this effort. She is trying to show how big her loss is, and almost everyone else is trying to minimize it. If you acknowledge this and respond to her with, "That must really hurt," then she has found someone who will understand and accept.

Establish the Significance of the Person

Did you notice how many of the family members of the victims after the terrorist attack on New York and the Pentagon would hold up large pictures of their loved ones? At first they did so hoping to find them alive. After the first few days, they did so hoping to find someone to talk with. Too often, when catastrophic tragedies happen, the surviving loved ones become one large group called "the families," and very few get to tell their stories. How can nearly three thousand families have the chance to tell about their loved ones? On our visits to New York after the tragedy, we spent most of our time listening to individual stories and looking at pictures. Survivors need someone to know the value of the person they lost.

In a small town in Texas, seven teenagers were killed in two car wrecks ten days apart. I was asked to help. I made several trips there before I ever put the families into a group. I wanted each family to have the chance to establish the individual significance of their child. No other story mattered.

Once again, most of the traditional efforts at giving comfort are counter to this need. The woman in our scenario wants to show how important the person is and how great the loss is and will be. Most people want to cheer her up by telling her that she will get past this and how good life will be. She feels trivialized once again.

If you come along, listen to her stories and talk about the person and the loss; your help matches her need.

Establish the Social Significance

We have funerals for this very purpose. A funeral is a time when friends can gather to grieve along with the loved ones and tell them how much the person meant to them. The longer I work with families in grief, the more value I see in the funeral, if that funeral is a personal expression about the life of the person. Too often funerals miss this need totally, but if they fit, they heal.

The woman needs to hear stories about her husband's friendship from others: times when they laughed together; times when he helped them in some way; things he said that they will always remember. All of these help her know that he will not be forgotten, that his life had meaning, and it will continue to do so long after he is gone. No one is dead until they are forgotten; she needs to know that he will be remembered.

When I say that people in grief need the Three H's, "Hang around" "Hug them" and "Hush," I am really saying that people simply need a safe person to get into their bucket and provide presence.

When one of his classmates died, an eight-year-old friend
visited the boy's home one day after school.
"What did you say?" asked his mother gently when
the child returned. "Nothing," he replied.
"I just sat on his mom's lap and helped her cry."

–Dan Zadra
Forever Remembered

Notes

_____

_____

_____

_____

_____

_____

_____

_____

_____

_____

_____

_____

_____

_____

_____

_____

_____

_____

_____

_____

_____

_____

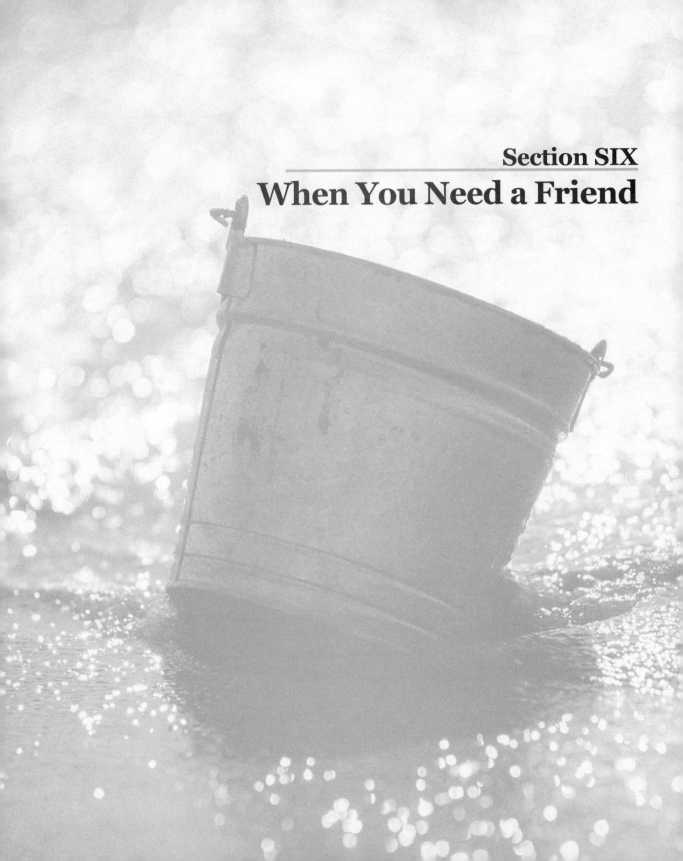

Section SIX

When You Need a Friend

Healthy personalities accept themselves not in any self-idolizing way, but in the sense that they see themselves as persons who are worth giving to another and worthy to receive from another.

–William Kalssen

When You Need A Friend

A professor in a school of mines asked his class to name the most important thing to ever come out of the mines. They guessed gold, silver, diamonds, and other valuable gems. The professor said they were all wrong. The most important thing to come out of the mines was the miner.

The most important issue in caregiving is caring for the caregivers. If you do not learn how to take care of yourself, you will not be able to give care to others for very long. The pressure will be too intense, and the work will become drudgery. The two most important questions you can answer are:

1.) What is in your bucket?

2.) Who gets in there with you?

May we look at those together?

All of us have feelings too deep for words. Feelings we would love to be able to discuss with someone. Feelings that make us wonder if we are not normal in some way. Feelings that make us wonder if other people feel the same way, or if they think the same things we think? These feelings and fears are always with us making us feel strange or different.

Maybe it would help if you paused and wrote out some of your feelings. You might want to use a code or abbreviations in case someone finds your notes. It helps to get them out and look at them in written form.

_____

_____

_____

_____

_____

_____

_____

_____

_____

_____

_____

_____

_____

_____

_____

_____

_____

What Are You Doing Now?

What are you doing now to combat the stress and fears you face? Most of us would have to write "not much" in answer to that question. We tend to ignore as much as possible for as long as possible. Trying to take action is frightening, and we must talk about and admit far too much, so we learn to fake it.

In caregiving, we learn to shift gears and go on. That was the world I lived in while serving in the ministry. I had to go from a sad funeral to a happy wedding. I learned to shift and go. The problem is, if that is the way we choose to deal with our feelings, we will get too good at it. We will get so good at shutting down that, ultimately, we will find it hard to feel anything at all. I have heard far too many people say they can't cry about anything anymore and then wonder what happened to them.

I tell clergy, nurses, doctors, hospice workers, funeral directors and others in caregiving professions that they can't cry at every funeral, but they need to cry at some of them. Shifting and going on is another word for denial and swallowing feelings.

Where Do You Go For Help?

Who helps you establish the significance of the things that happen to you? Who gets in your bucket? Everyone needs a support system. That does not mean you must join a support group that meets every Tuesday. It just means we all need some place to vent. We all need someplace where we can let our feet stink, a place of safety, a place where we do not have to perform or fake anything, a place where we can keep our cussing current.

The premise of this book is that support comes in human form. We cannot find outlets in caves nor comfort in the wind. It takes people. It takes safe people. It takes people willing and brave enough to get in our buckets.

If we do not have an outlet for these feelings and we are involved in some intense world of caring for others, we are likely to burnout. I am an expert on burnout. I burned out in the ministry. I came home one night and told my wife I would rather die than have to attend one more deacon's meeting.

Burnout is insidious. It slips up on us. It seems to be a gradual, unnoticed build-up that suddenly hits with a vengeance. It does not have to be so. There are many red flags that warn us of impending problems. Burnout is a gradual loss in some very evident areas.

Gradual Loss Of Ideals

We begin to be more and more cynical. We think everyone is on the take. I began to think everyone was going to hell, and I was rather glad they were. We need to check our cynicism rate like we check the oil in our cars.

All of us get up on certain mornings, and we do not like anyone. That is normal. However, if this feeling persists over a period of time, we need to recognize that as a red flag warning us of some needs in our lives. It means you need a break for some intense self care.

Gradual Loss Of Purpose

We begin to go through the motions. We do our job almost automatically with very little interest or joy. I started preaching because it was eleven o'clock on Sunday not because I had anything to say nor cared whether or not my congregation heard it.

There is a form of depression that does not exemplify itself by feeling blue or low; it exemplifies itself by *no* feelings. We feel flat and detached. We seem to be standing off watching ourselves go though motions without any response from us.

We all have days when we have no feelings, when we just go through motions and have no emotional responses to anything. That, too, is normal, but if it persists, then we need to notice and find a way to empty the bucket.

Gradual Loss Of Humor

Things are no longer funny. Things we once would not even notice now hurt our feelings. We begin to make mountains out of molehills and cannot seem to stop ourselves. We get up every morning already irritated, and it does not get any better all day. That is a red flag.

Gradual Loss Of Energy

We can't seem to get rested. I often say that in Oklahoma we have two words. We have "tired," and we have "tard." I was "tard" all of the time. I just could not find the energy I once had. Sleep did not make me feel rested. It was as if I was carrying around a huge burden, and I could not lay it down or find a way to rest while it was there.

Gradual Loss Of Morals

I now understand more about why so many well-known ministers got involved in affairs or other unexpected alliances. When I was burned out, I could justify things I have never been able to justify before or since.

The burned out mind plays tricks on us. It says, "Everyone is taking from me, and no one is putting anything back. Everyone wants something from me; when do I get mine?" There is always someone there who will give you yours. I am convinced that most of the affairs that men have after the age of forty-five have nothing to do with love or sex and everything to do with burnout. Someone came by to give them what they thought they needed, and they did not have to face up to that need nor did they have to find any help.

Identifying the Causes

We not only need to learn how to find outlets for our feelings, we also need to find new ways of relating to those we work with or live with.

Notice the three columns on the next page.

Under "Stress" write in the natural stresses of life—the things we all face, the mechanical things that are just part of living: time restraints, money worries, health worries, job security, weather, traffic, and other stress producers of that type. These are the inevitable stresses we all must face. No one causes them to happen; they are just the normal result of living.

Under "Tension" write out all of the people that cause tension in your life; those who jerk a knot in your stomach when you are around them; those who make you feel inadequate; those who make you angry; those who are unfair in their judgments of you. These may be spouses, children, in-laws, bosses, co-workers, and anyone else you can think of. These are the sources of the tensions in your life.

If you attend a stress management seminar, you are taught to do such things as relax, meditate, manage time, give yourself TLC, exercise, and other techniques. These are wonderful, and they are important, but they only work on stress. They do not work on tension. The only thing that works on tension is learning how to get people off of our backs.

I do not have any magic cure. I have grown weary of guaranteed cures for the things that ail us. Since we are dealing with people, nothing is going to work every time, nor is it going to work on everybody. I do have something to try that has worked on a lot of people.

Stress	Tension	Self

Hooks

Most of your tension comes from being manipulated by someone. Others learn how to say just the right things to put you down or make you look foolish. I call that "Hooks." We learn how to hook one another. We were raised on hooks. Most of our mothers were masters at the craft. I saw my wife hook my granddaughter. They were making a dress so the granddaughter could be in a wedding. The granddaughter would not stand still so my wife could pin the dress. So my wife said, "Well, I guess we will not have a dress." The granddaughter got tears in her eyes and said she wanted a dress. My wife then told her to stand still, and she did. That is a hook, well presented and well bitten.

We use all kinds of hooks in our lives. Little "hinty" hooks like the man I know that waited until his wife was close enough to hear and said to the dog, "I guess you are the only one around here that loves me." Never-fail hooks. Marriages don't have fights; they have a fight—the same one over and over. No matter what the fight starts about, it will head for the hooks that work. A friend of mine can get his wife everytime by saying, "You never have liked my folks." The wife always loses it and says, "How could you say that? I have always been great to your parents." The truth is she really doesn't like them, but even if she did, he could never admit it. If he admits it, he loses the hook that he can always count on.

There are the "get down and get dirty" hooks. I listened to a couple fight in the next room of a motel late one night. I could not sleep, so I sat on the side of the bed and called the fight. The wife began to win, and I knew something was getting ready to happen. Although it had nothing to do with the fight, the husband said, "It wasn't me that had an abortion." I could hear the wind go out of her. She cried for a long time and then said, "You have promised me and promised me never to say that again. You were part of that decision. Why do you keep throwing it in my face?" He does so because it works. People will hook you as long as you bite.

There really are only three hooks. They are guilt, fear, and anger. The strange thing is, people will usually use them in that order. First they will try to make you feel guilty. If that doesn't work, they will try to make you fearful. If that doesn't work, they will either try to make you lose yourself in anger, or they will get angry.

The good news is that people who are skilled as listeners are the hardest people to manipulate. They are focused on hearing instead of talking, so they see the hooks coming. Most people bite the hook and then see it a day or so later. Individuals with good listening skills don't feel the need to rebut every thing that is said. They can see the hooks for what they are. If we can see them, we have a much better chance of disarming them.

I make a game of it. When someone starts trying to hook me, I notice and think, "That is the "guilt" one. I wonder how they will do the fear one?" When the fear hook is going on, I wonder if they are going to get mad or if I am supposed to do that. It is amazing to me how seeing what is really going on can help us avoid falling into the same traps.

We need to learn how to say, "Tell someone who cares," or "I am sorry you feel that way, but I don't feel the same as you." I have told many people, "If I made a mistake, it is my mistake, and I have the right to determine how guilty I am going to feel about that."

If you are in a relationship that lives on hooks and you quit biting, get ready for some real "hookerization" to happen. People only give up hooks when it is evident they will absolutely never work again. The great thing is that when the hooks are gone, real communication can begin.

What About Self

The third column is what we put on ourselves. I wish I could produce an entire book on how much pain we cause for ourselves. We feel inferior because we tell ourselves we are. We tend to put ourselves down and be overcritical about almost every part of who we are. If you would take a moment and write out all of the negative things you put on you, it would be amazing.

I had to realize something important about me. I said that when I was burned out I thought everyone was taking from me and no one was putting anything back. I had to realize that no one was putting back because I would not let them do so. Getting into someone's bucket is scary, but it is also scary letting someone into ours. As soon as someone says "How are you?", we tend to hide our bucket behind our backs and say we are fine. The fear of intimacy can close us off from even the safe people who want to help. Most of us spend our lives hiding our buckets and talking about how we want to be close to people. It takes great courage to face the fear of exposure and vulnerability and let some other person into our bucket. Relief from stress waits on that courage.

I have what I call *Caregiver Syndrome.* Every caregiver I know has some of that. Some of us have a lot of it. Caregiver Syndrome means we get very good at giving care, but we never learn how to receive any. To a person with Caregiver Syndrome, the hardest part of love is not loving; it is being loved by letting someone in your bucket.

I can listen all night to someone's pain. I can even talk with him about dying. The problem is, I would most likely never tell him about my own pain. I only know how to give. I don't know how to receive.

Those of us afflicted with this malady love to hear people tell us we are doing too much. That is like saying "sic 'em" to a bull dog. We will work ourselves to death so they will say it again. We get all of our self-esteem out of giving. That is the only time we feel good about ourselves.

Letting others help us makes us feel vulnerable. We want to give the blessing. We don't want to be the one who is blessed. That is Caregiver's Syndrome.

If we have it, we are lonely, because we never allow anyone inside where our hurts are. We must be in control and safe.

My brother and I were best friends. The day he died I was in Atlanta, Georgia. I called California, where he lived, to check on him on a Tuesday afternoon about 1:00 Atlanta time. He died while I was on the phone. I had to make a speech at 4:00 and another one at 7:30. I made them both, and no one ever knew my brother had died. I went to dinner between the two speeches and did not tell anyone about my loss. I did not want them to feel sorry for me.

I was scheduled to stay in Atlanta on Wednesday and be interviewed on CNN Thursday morning. I made all of the necessary flight arrangements so I could do that interview and leave Atlanta at noon on Thursday to meet my wife and mother in route and get to California that night. The funeral was to be the next day. I went to bed that night with all the plans in place. To a person with Caregiver Syndrome, the show must go on.

I woke in the night and realized that I did not want to stay and work. I wanted to go home, and, for the first time in my life, I did not want to take care of anybody. I did not want to be strong. I wanted someone to take care of me. I wanted to cry and be weak. I caught the first plane home the next morning. That was the healthiest day of my life. It is not enough to love. It is only enough when you know how to be loved in return and allow someone to be in your bucket.

To laugh often and much
To win the respect of intelligent people and
the affection of children
To earn the appreciation of honest critics and
endure the betrayal of false friends;
To appreciate beauty
To find the best in others
To leave the world a bit better, whether by a healthy child,
a garden patch or a redeemed social condition
To know that even one life has breathed
easier because you lived
That is to have succeeded.

–Ralph Waldo Emerson

Notes

Guide for Facilitators

This book can be used as a training guide for many people: hospice workers, funeral home directors, nursing home workers, church lay ministries, chaplains, anyone who will be walking with people in pain.

We are providing some guidelines and suggested discussion questions to help plan a series of training sessions. You may decide how they apply to your audience and how to adapt them to fit your needs.

Setting

Any training session is dependent upon the setting and comfort level established for the participants. Assuring that your setting is in a place with minimal distractions or interruptions and a place where participants feel free to share will go a long way to providing a successful session.

It is always important to allow time for participants to "get their voice in the room." Whether that means introductions, sharing experiences, or reflecting on the previous session—it is vital that each person has a chance to speak and be spoken to.

Three Basic Principles for Trainers of Adults:
1. The Environment must promote interaction, informality, and comfort:
    - Round tables
    - Refreshments
    - Room to move around
    - Reliable starting and ending times

2. The Climate must be open, nonthreatening, and pleasant
   - Address anxieties or concerns
   - Urge participation and involvement
   - Use accumulated experiences as a springboard for discussion
3. The Task must be relevant
   - Relate the topic to their experiences
   - Watch for "furrowed" brows
   - Devote time to questions and other points of view

Adult Learners have some unique qualities that every facilitator needs to keep in mind:
- Adults see themselves as self-directing, responsible grown-ups.
- Adults have more experience and more to contribute.
- Adults are predisposed to learn from life's problems. They seek practical results from learning.
- Adults learn by doing and by the use of a variety of methods.
- Adults must want to learn. They chose to come to the training, and it may be wise to check out why they came and what they are seeking.
- Adult learning is an ongoing and continuous process.
- Adult learning can be threatening when it means change
- Adults learn best in an informal environment.

Tools

To help visualize the "buckets" scenarios, it might be helpful to have either one set of buckets at the front of the group or small individual buckets for each participant. These can be found at most hardware or hobby stores.

As the trainer, it is important that you have already gone through each of the scenarios and written out your responses, so you will be familiar with the questions and comfortable with reactions you might receive from participants.

There are several ways to approach the presentation.
- Assign a section to be read before the session and ask the participants to write their responses to the scenarios and be ready to share their responses.
- Lead a discussion about the section and leave time for the participants to write responses and share.
- Lead a discussion about the section and ask the participants to write responses away from the group before the next session.

Section One

This is a long section that could be broken into several sessions, if necessary.

Can We Talk?

1. Can you identify a specific time when you were faced with a person in pain and found you were uncomfortable or unsure how to respond?
2. Which of the scenarios most closely fit situations that you find yourself in on a regular basis?
3. How did the bucket visualization help you focus on what people might be feeling?
4. What was the best insight you gained from this section, and how can you utilize it?

Ears and Learning/Laying Ears on 'Em

1. Are you an "innie" or an "outie"?
2. Can you identify situations where it was very difficult to listen and let the person in pain find insight while talking?

3. Does the concept of trivialization ring true for you? How?
4. Can you recognize when a person is trying to establish the significance of an event? How?
5. Can you recognize the pattern outlined—explain, argue, and criticize?
6. Have you found yourself in that pattern when dealing with people?
7. What is the best insight you gained from this section, and how can you utilize it?

The Healing Pattern

1. Of the three issues outlined—comfort, focus, and timing— which one do you think is the biggest challenge when you work with people?
2. What issues did you identify for the bucket of the woman whose mother is in the nursing home?
3. What issues did you identify for the nursing home administrator?
4. Which bucket is more closely aligned with how you feel in working with people?
5. What is the best insight you gained from this section, and how can you utilize it?

The Personal Bucket

1. Can you identify situations in your work or personal life in which using the bucket concept would improve communication?
2. How difficult is it to apply these principles closer to home?
3. What is the best insight you gained from this section, and how can you utilize it?

Section Two
When Youth Has Fled

1. What new perceptions did you gain from this section?
2. Do you deal with people in this situation in your work?
3. From your experience, does the description of how the aging are not allowed to deal with their pain seem accurate?
4. What is the best insight you gained from this section, and how can you utilize it?

Section Three
When Care Must Be Given

1. Does this describe people you are working with who are caregivers for aging or ill loved ones?
2. Have you found people who become overwhelmed or obsessed with caregiving?
3. What is the best method for getting in caregivers' buckets?
4. What is the best insight you gained from this section, and how can you utilize it?

Section Four
When Death Draws Near

1. Have you been in the situation of being with a person who is dying?
2. Have you seen the "fear of speaking it out loud" family reactions?
3. How did that affect the patient? How did it affect the family?
4. What bucket issues did you identify for yourself in the scenario of being a terminally ill person ?
5. What bucket issues did you identify for a loved one?

6. What bucket issues did you identify for the response from a clergy person?
7. What is the best insight you gained from this section, and how can you utilize it?

Section Five
When Grief Overwhelms

1. What areas in the description of grief were most helpful to you in thinking about the people you work with?
2. Which specific death situations are the ones you must deal with the most?
3. How do you think grieving people find "safe" people?
4. Have you struggled with being with a person and allowing his anger to be expressed? How difficult was it for you?
5. Have you experienced people trying to establish the significance of their loss?
6. Have you experienced people trying to establish the significance of the person they lost?
7. Have you experienced people trying to establish the social significance of the person they lost?
8. What issues or skills did you identify that can be used to help people in grief establish significance?
9. What is the best insight you gained from this section, and how can you utilize it?

Section Six
When You Need A Friend

1. Was this the most difficult section for you to experience?
2. Why do you think it is more difficult to identify your own needs and losses rather than focusing on the people with whom you work?

3. Do you identify with the concept of "hooks"?
4. Have you experienced people trying to "hook" you?
5. Do you identify with the concept of "caregiver syndrome"?
6. What types of interventions have you tried to avoid burnout?
7. What has been successful? What has not worked?
8. What is the best insight you gained from this section, and how can you utilize?

General Overview

1. Will the concept of "getting in other people's buckets" be something that reminds you to focus and use listening skills when working with people in pain?
2. What will be the most difficult challenge for you in working with people?
3. What will be the most rewarding challenge for you in working with people?
4. What avenues or attitudes do you think can be changed for people going through this training?
5. What is the best insight you gained from this book/training?

Doug Manning

His career has included minister, counselor, business executive, author and publisher. He and his wife, Barbara, have been parents to four daughters and long-term caregivers to three parents.

After thirty years in the ministry, Doug began a new career in 1982. He now devotes his time to writing, counseling, and leading seminars in the areas of grief and elder care. His publishing company, In-Sight Books, Inc., specializes in books, video, and audio tapes specifically designed to help people face some of the toughest challenges of life.

Doug has a warm, conversational style in which he shares insights from his various experiences. Sitting down to read a book from Doug is like having a long conversation with a good friend.

Selected Resources from In-Sight Books

by Doug Manning
Grief

Don't Take My Grief Away From Me
The Special Care Series
Lean On Me Gently: Helping the Grieving Child
Thoughts for the Lonely Nights
Thoughts for the Grieving Christian
The Funeral: A Chance to Touch, A Chance to Serve, A Chance to Heal
Thoughts for the Holidays: Permission to Grieve

Elder Care

Aging is a Family Affair
The Gifts You Bring Series
Parenting Our Parents
Searching for Normal Feelings
Share My Lonesome Valley: The Slow Grief of Long-Term Care
Socks: How to Solve Problems
Visiting in a Nursing Home
When Love Gets Tough: The Nursing Home Decision

Other Resources from In-Sight Books

I Know Someone Who Died coloring book by Connie Manning
The Empty Chair: The Journey of Grief After Suicide by Beryl Glover
The Shattered Dimension: The Journey of Grief After Suicide video with
     Beryl Glover
Comfort Cards

In-Sight Books, Inc.
Helping People Help People

For a complete catalog or ordering information:
800-658-9262 or 405-810-9501
www.insightbooks.com
orders&info@insightbooks.com